Letters from Maine

New Poems

Books by May Sarton

Letters from Maine

New Poems
By MAY SARTON

W · W · NORTON & COMPANY
New York · London

Published simultaneously in Canada by
Penguin Books Canada Ltd,
2801 John Street, Markham, Ontario L3R 1B4.

Printed in the United States of America.

The text of this book is composed in Janson, with display type set in Deepdene.
Composition and manufacturing by The Maple-Vail Book Manufacturing Group.

Library of Congress Cataloging in Publication Data
Sarton, May, 1912–
    Letters from Maine.
    I. Title.
PS3537.A832L4   1984   811'.52   84–1123

ISBN 0-393-01941-1

ISBN 0-393-30222-9 pbk.

W. W. Norton & Company, Inc., 500 Fifth Avenue, New York, N. Y. 10110
W. W. Norton & Company Ltd., 37 Great Russell Street, London WC1B 3NU

    4 5 6 7 8 9 0

Contents

Part III Letters to Myself

Some of these poems first appeared in *American Journal*, *The Bennington Review*, *Blue Unicorn*, *Black Willow*, *Choomia*, *The Hampton-Sydney Poetry Review*, *Negative Capability*, *The Paris Review*, *The Virginia Quarterly Review*, *WEID*.

The section, *A Winter Garland*, was published in a limited edition by William B. Ewert in 1982.

Letters from Maine

New Poems

Contemplation of Poussin

From symptoms of disaster, blight, and woe
Where all within is muddied and unclear,
Romantic impulse stained like dirty snow,
My desk, chaotic, no order even there,
No sanctity within my mind to bless
Or to redeem a cannibal distress—

The furious tears spring up from below
Where reason cannot touch their source.
Uprooted love, contempt (that dirtied snow)
Struggle to deal with an unspoken curse,
Romantic impulse turned against itself,
Snake biting its tail. I'm torn in half.

I eat myself. Where find the will to break
Off from the futile game of hearts,
What trick to free the old self-eating snake,
Uncoil the misery? You healing arts,
Mozart, come back, Poussin, come to redeem
And change the light within this somber room!

Under a wild tumultuous sky I see
A goat, a lute, wine, and a mask
Where men and women drink to end their pain
And Poussin brings together as I ask
Romantic impulse, classic symmetry
Married in the holistic mystery.

Without the wine, without the wild-eyed goat
Where would creation start, or generate?
Without the serene lady with her lute
How would lust be transformed to sacred fruit?
Without the mask what art could learn to show
A naked heart alive, fire under the snow?

Celestial harmony would never move
Us earthlings if it had not sprung from blood.
The source flows bright from every carnal love.
Poussin has come to tell me what is good
And find the blessing in some artful play.
Apollo once more shines the dark away.

Part I

Letters from Maine

A Farewell

For a while I shall still be leaving,
Looking back at you as you slip away
Into the magic islands of the mind.
But for a while now all alive, believing
That in a single poignant hour
We did say all that we could ever say
In a great flowing out of radiant power.
It was like seeing and then going blind.

After a while we shall be cut in two
Between real islands where you live
And a far shore where I'll no longer keep
The haunting image of your eyes, and you,
As pupils widen, widen to deep black
And I am able neither to love or grieve
Between fulfillment and heartbreak.
The time will come when I can go to sleep.

But for a while still, centered at last,
Contemplate a brief amazing union,
Then watch you leave and then let you go.
I must not go back to the murderous past
Nor force a passage through to some safe landing,
But float upon this moment of communion
Entranced, astonished by pure understanding—
Passionate love dissolved like summer snow.

Letters from Maine

1

Yes, I am home again, and alone.
Today wrote letters then took my dog
Out through the sad November woods.
The leaves have fallen while I was away,
The ground is golden while above
The maples are stripped of all color.
The ornamental cherries, red when I left,
Have paled now to translucent yellow.

Yes, I am home again, but home has changed.
And I within this cultivated space
That I have made my own, feel at a loss,
Disoriented. All the safe doors
Have come unlocked and too much light
Has flooded every room. Where can I go?
Not toward you three thousand miles away
Lost in your own rich life, given me
For an hour.
           Read between the lines.
Then meet me in the silence if you can,
The long silence of winter when I shall
Make poems out of nothing, out of loss,
And at times hear your healing laughter.

2

November opens the sky. I look out
On an immense perimeter of ocean, blue
On every side, through the great oak
That screens it off all summer, see surf
Edging the rocks white on the other side.
The November muse who is with me now
Gives me wisdom and laughter, also clarity.
Aware of old age for the first time, accept
That I am old, and this sudden passion must be
A single sharp cry, torn out of me, as when
A few days ago on the ferry to Vancouver
I saw an eagle fly down in a great arc,
His fierce head flashing white among the gulls.
The ardor of seventy years seizes the moment
And must be held free, outside time,
Must learn to bear with the cleared space,
The futureless flame, and use it well,
Must rejoice in the still, quiet air
And this ineluctable solitude.

3

No letter from the muse. Time out.
Nevertheless I am floated on her presence,
Her strong reality, swung out above
Everything else that happens. In the mail
News of two brutal murders, and a wedding,
News of a poet friend in deep depression,
News from strangers reading my poems
And comforted, they say. I am suspended,
Wake before dawn to watch the sun come
Up from leaden waters every morning.
Turning the whole sky orange as it rises.
Slowly I learn the self who is emerging
As though newborn after a sterile summer.
Alone? Perhaps. But filled to the brim
With all that comes and goes, rejoicing.

Now there is someone to hold the kite
As it is tossed by the wind, keep it floating.
I manage better than I have for months to be
Open and balanced. The muse is there
To let the kite fly as high as it can,
Then slowly draw it in when there is peril.
So many times this summer it was broken,
Caught up in a tree or unable to fly.
The kite, marvelous muse, is in your hands.

4

There was your voice, astonishment,
Falling into the silence suddenly
As though there were no continent
Between its warmth and me at my desk,
Bringing joy to the roots, a giant gift
Across time. Five in the morning there.
Three thousand miles to cover instantly.
How is it done? How for that matter
Did it all happen when we met?
Time telescoped, years cast away,
And primal being finding this present
Where we were lifted beyond age,
Outside responsibilities, newfound,
In a way stranded, in a way home at last?
And in your tender laughter at me
Some total acceptance of all that I am,
Of all that is to be or not ever to be
As time goes on and we are lost
Or found in it over and over again.

5

From a distance the ocean looks calm,
Gray and unbroken stretching out to Spain,
But it is seamed with hidden tumult.
The long swells come in slowly from below
And build to immense fluid walls
Driven in by some deep pulse far away,
Ominous while they stand suspended
Then at the rock edge tumble, broken,
And send up shattered towers of white foam.
Muse, do you feel the tumult over there?
Or is it only steadfastness of mountains
Today that holds you still and silent?
While I, like one of the black ducks
Bobbing out there, must keep my balance,
Stay clear of the rocks as they do
Who know how to ride this tumult safely
And play its perils like a game.

6

"When a woman feels alone, when the room
Is full of daemons," the Nootka tribe
Tells us, "The Old Woman will be there."
She has come to me over three thousand miles
And what does she have to tell me, troubled
"by phantoms in the night?" Is she really here?
What is the saving word from so deep in the past,
From as deep as the ancient root of the redwood,
From as deep as the primal bed of the ocean,
From as deep as a woman's heart sprung open
Again through a hard birth or a hard death?
Here under the shock of love, I am open
To you, Primal Spirit, one with rock and wave,
One with the survivors of flood and fire,
Who have rebuilt their homes a million times,
Who have lost their children and borne them again.
The words I hear are *strength, laughter, endurance.*
Old Woman I meet you deep inside myself.
There in the rootbed of fertility,
World without end, as the legend tells it.
Under the words you are my silence.

7

Who has spoken of the unicorn in old age?
She who was hunted for her strangeness,
Androgynous, fleeing her pursuers, hopeful
When she was young that she could bow her horn
Before the perfect innocence and purity
Of a virgin being. Who has wondered
Whether she did find shelter at last?
Or does she wander still, searching human faces
For the one who might speak of her
In her own language, look into her eyes
And gentle the wildness once and for all?
It may be that through that fervent pursuit
The unicorn has come to look for wisdom
And experience rather than innocence,
That she looks for a woman who has suffered
And become like gold, the dross beaten out,
As round and whole as a wedding ring,
A woman who has laughed and wept her way
Through the dark wood and across the lake,
Who has borne children, and who is now
Marvelously open, transparent, and unafraid.
Who has imagined the unicorn grown old?

8

When I heard you say in a brisk voice
"Perhaps we should never meet again,"
The sun turned black, the tide froze,
I could feel the blood withering in my veins,
A breakdown of cells, death in my body.
It took an instant, three thousand miles,
And your voice alive in the room, to do it.
And now after days muffled in distress,
I must try to speak words when the reality
Is an immense silence, and nothing can be said.

Perhaps it is, after all, delusion and madness,
The poet forcing her muse to pay attention,
Forcing too much out of an hour of bliss,
Unable "to take love lightly as the grass
Grows on the weirs," trying to hold back the tide
From ebbing into the deeps. Not possible.

Nevertheless is my answer to your *never*.
Whatever the reasons they are only reason.
And here in the universe of souls
Reason is not the master of the moment,
Was not when we met and stared into each other's eyes
Like sleepers woken suddenly out of a dream,
Suffering a blaze of light. Was that madness?
Was it delusion? No, a gift from the goddess.
Nothing is possible. Nothing is real, you think.
Nevertheless . . . nevertheless . . . nevertheless . . .

9

The muse of course airs out the inner world,
Without her presence somewhere a cell
With no window, where the poet struggles,
Snake biting its tail, Narcissus
Drowned in his own image. The muse
Ripples the waters, opens doors,
Lets in sunlight, dazzles and delights.
She frees the poet from all obligations,
Guilt, doubt, to wander alone by the sea
Picking up shells, or contemplating mosses
In the woods, free to be herself, to sing,
Uncontaminated by duties, projected outward,
Able to pay attention to the smallest stir
Of wind in the silence, to observe birds.

When the muse appears after long absence
Everything stops except the poem. It rises
In an unbroken wave and topples to silence.
There is no way to make it happen by will.
No muse appears when invoked, dire need
Will not rouse her pity.
                    She comes when she can,
She too, no doubt, rising from the sea
Like Aphrodite on her shell when it is time,
When the impersonal tide bears her to the shore
To play a difficult role she has not chosen,
To free a prisoner she has no reason to love.

What power is at work, then, what key
Opens the door into these mysteries?

10

The muse is here, she who dazzled the air
For months at a distance now gives her presence
To this house, lies on the terrace wrapped
In her own thoughts, an icy visage, silent.
No harsh or tender word could now unblind her.
She has chosen not to see and even not to be,
Medusa who has frozen herself into a trance.

It happened too long ago, should have been buried
Then like a meteor fallen in an open field,
Having no usefulness except as a sample
Of what goes on occasionally in the sky,
Indifferent to human affairs. Yet she came
Who knows for what purpose? She is here.

All day amenities fall on my head like hail.
The house is a black hole. At night I know
The muse as Medusa plays her cruel games
But cannot blight the center where I live,
And where I know, have always known, the paths
Of grace cannot be forced, yet meteors will fall,
A blaze of light, and always when least looked for.
So deal with absence. Survivors learn it.
Eat grass. I know my way on barren islands,
Lie down on rock at night and read the stars.

Never curse the curse, or forget the blessing.
Since all things move together to grave ends
We need not even ask where we are bound.

Let the muse bury the dead. For that she came.
Who walks the earth in joy and poverty?
Who then has risen? The tomb is empty.

Part II

A Winter Garland

Twelve Below

A bitter gale
Over frozen snow
Burns the skin like hail.
It is twelve below.

Too cold to live
Too cold to die
Warm animals wait
And make no cry.

Their feathers puff
Their eyes are bright
Their fur expands.
Warm animals wait.

They make no sign
They waste no breath
In this cold country
Between life and death.

Dead Center

Temperature zero, the road an icy glare,
The field, once ermine soft, now hard and bright.
Even my cat's paws find no footing there.
And I sit watching barren winter sunlight
Travel the empty house. I sit and stare.

This is dead center. There is no escape,
And like the starving deer I must survive
On what each day may bring of somber hope—
For them, a hidden yew. They keep alive.
For me, a letter to soften the grim landscape.

Beyond this frozen world the ocean lies
Immense, impersonal, and calm,
Perimeter I measure with my eyes.
To the horizon's rim it is blue balm,
Dark lively blue under the wan skies.

This is dead center. I am the one
Who holds it in myself, the one who sees
And can contain ocean and sky and sun
And keep myself alive in the deep freeze
With a warm uncontaminated vision.

Temperature zero, and death on my mind.
I contemplate the earthquakes and the fears,
The leaps into the dark, lovers unkind,
The wild hopes and the damaged atmospheres.
They could not stop the blood or make me blind.

It is all in myself, hope and despair.
The heartbeat never stops. The veins are filled
And my warm blood in the cold winter air
Will not be frozen or be winter-killed.
Poetry comes back with the starving deer.

Shell

Outside,
The sea's susurration,
Inside,
A terrible silence
As though everything had died,
One of those shells
Abandoned by the creature
Who lived there once
And opened to the tide.

Lift it to an ear
And you will hear
A long reverberation
In its tiny cave,
The rumor of a wave
Long ago broken
And drawn back
Into the ocean—
And so, with love.

Correspondence

Faces at the window
Am I never to be without you?
Cries for help in the night
Am I never to sleep?

Why do I feel compelled
To answer, day after day,
Answer the stranger
At the window?
In the hope that shared pain
Can become healing?
That if I spend myself
Without stint
I shall be made whole?
That the long woe
Will come to an end?
Or the gift come back—
Poetry, forgiveness?

Faces at the window
Am I never to be without you?
Cries for help in the night
Am I never to sleep?

I have no more springs
No living water
For your spent wells,
I am stiff and frozen
In the winter ice.

It is time I heard
My own voice weeping,
Felt the warm tears
Of absolution
On my icy cheek.
It is time you let me sleep

The unhealable
Into the dark.

But how to do it?
It would take a pickaxe now
To break through to the source.

Snow Fall

With no wind blowing
It sifts gently down,
Enclosing my world in
A cool white down,
A tenderness of snowing.

It falls and falls like sleep
Till wakeful eyes can close
On all the waste and loss
As peace comes in and flows,
Snow-dreaming what I keep.

Silence assumes the air
And the five senses all
Are wafted on the fall
To somewhere magical
Beyond hope and despair.

There is nothing to do
But drift now, more or less
On some great lovingness,
On something that does bless,
The silent, tender snow.

For Monet

Poets, too, are crazed by light,
How to capture its changes,
How to be accurate in seizing
What has been caught by the eye
In an instant's flash—
Light through a petal,
Iridescence of clouds before sunrise.
They, too, are haunted by the need
To hold the fleeting still
In a design—
That vermillion under the haystack,
Struck at sunset,
Melting into the golden air
Yet perfectly defined,
An illuminated transience.

Today my house is lost in milk,
The milky veils of a blizzard.
The trees have turned pale.
There are no shadows.
That is the problem—no shadows
At all.

It is harder to see what one sees
Than anyone knows.
Monet knew, spent a lifetime
Trying to undazzle the light
And pin it down.

The Cold Night

In the time of great tension and of splendor,
I knew not whether I was joy or grief,
Whether swung out on madness or belief,
Or some difficult truth to bend—or
Whether it was the relentless thrust
Of withheld poetry bursting my chest.
But in the time of splendor was alone
In a strange land of fire and broken stone,
And the long fading light across bright snow,
Until if you did speak, I did not know,
Caught up by some angelic voice or choir
Under huge skies where shone no single star.
Now all is silence. Where have you gone
Whose heartbeat did reverberate through stone?

Listen, listen! The wild foxes bark.
Venus is rising, tranquil, through the dark.

Seascape

In endless variations on a theme
The waves come in and lace the rocky shore.
One after one long ripples rise and spread
Until they break in necklaces of foam
Or fountain up in spume, an endless store—
The gentle sea is singing in my head.

High in my study I look down and through
The great oak and its branches naked now.
They accent the whole scene and unify
With strong black lines blue against paler blue,
And in the foreground shadow the late snow.
Spring in the air has come to rinse my eye.

Newly aware and open to the scene
I hold fast to the little I can hold,
A long continuum so like the play
Of the incessant waves, unbroken theme
Of love, love without a fold
Murmuring under silence like the sea.

After a Winter's Silence

Along the terrace wall
Snowdrops have pushed through
Hard ice, making a pool.
Delicate stems now show
White bells as though
The force, the thrust to flower
Were nothing at all.
Who gives them the power?

After a winter's silence
I feel the shock of spring.
My breath warms like the sun,
Melts ice, bursts into song.
So when that inner one
Gives life back the power
To rise up and push through,
There's nothing to it.
We simply have to do it,
As snowdrops know
When snowdrops flower.

Moose in the Morning

Oh wild and gentle beast,
Immense antlered shape,
This morning in the meadow!
Like something ancient, lost
And found now, promise kept,
Emerging from the shadow,
Emerging while I slept—
Wilderness and escape!
You set me free to shirk
The day's demanding work
And cast my guilt away.
You make a truant of me
This moose-enchanted day
When all I can is *see*,
When all I am is this
Astonishment and bliss.

The Wood Pigeons

The wood pigeons
Punctuate the silence
With coos, over and over,
Over and over,
One long, three shorts,
Then pause,
Then resume.

Nothing else moves
Or makes a sound,
Flat blue sky
Over silent shining sea.
Peace
Interrupted
By the wood pigeons
Insistent, monotonous
"Spring is coming
Spring is coming."
Coo, coo-coo.

How can we stand it?
Madness is in the air.

Elegy:
The Rose-Breasted Grosbeak

My evening delight
Is dead, torn apart,
His crimson breast,
His black and white,
Who had been my guest,
Whom I fed, whom I blest.
Cat ate his heart.

How to bear the blow
In the house alone.
The blight of murder,
Fall of the shadow?
Cat was the killer.
It is her nature—
But how to atone?

What beauty be kept
From the wheel's turn?
What saved from the curse?
How can I accept
Nature's bloody course
For better or worse?
I can't. I must mourn

For death in the spring.
For the bright one lost,
He who perched so near
With his blue-black wing,
He who knew no fear
(Oh my dear, my dear)
For his crimson breast.

April in Maine

The days are cold and brown,
Brown fields, no sign of green,
Brown twigs, not even swelling,
And dirty snow in the woods.

But as the dark flows in
The tree frogs begin
Their shrill sweet singing,
And we lie on our beds
Through the ecstatic night,
Wide awake, cracked open.

There will be no going back.

Part III

Letters to Myself

For Laurie

The people she loved are leaving
Her one by one
And she is left with the grieving,
Herself alone.

Herself who wakes in the morning
Now it is May
Like a small child mourning
A lost day.

Herself and the mountain near,
Ancient friend,
Herself in her ninetieth year
When lilacs bend

Under their weight of bloom
And ninety springs
Flow through her upstairs room,
And memory sings.

Alive to the loving past
She conjures her own.
Nothing is wholly lost—
Sun on the stone.

And lilacs in their splendor
Like lost friends
Come back through grief to tell her
Love never ends.

Mourning to Do

The new year and a fresh fall of snow,
The new year and mourning to do
Alone here in the lovely silent house,
Alone as the inner eye opens at last—
Not as the shutter of a camera with a click,
But like a gentle waking in a dark room
Before dawn when familiar objects take on
Substance out of their shadowy corners
And come to life. So with my lost love,
For years lost in the darkness of her mind,
Tied to a wheelchair, not knowing where she was
Or who she had been when we lived together
In amity, peaceful as turtledoves.

Judy is dead.   Judy is gone forever.

I cannot fathom that darkness, nor know
Whether the true spirit is alive again.
But what I do know is the peace of it,
And in the darkened room before dawn, I lie
Awake and let the good tears flow at last,
And as light touches the chest of drawers
And the windows grow transparent, rest,
Happy to be mourning what was singular
And comforting as the paintings on the wall,
All that can now come to life in my mind,
Good memories fresh and sweet as the dawn—
Judy drinking her tea with a cat on her lap,
And our many little walks before suppertime.
So it is now the gentle waking to what was,
And what is and will be as long as I am alive.
"Happy grieving," someone said who knew—
Happy the dawn of memory and the sunrise.

Survivors

What they dreamed,
Lying on filthy mattresses
Was to bear witness,
To tell, to make known,
To sanctify horror
By bringing it into the open world
To be cleansed and purified
By human tears . . .
Each survivor, a miracle,
To be greeted like Lazarus
Anointed and cherished.
This is what kept them alive.

A handful survived
Holding the dream in their arms,
But they learned
When their mouths opened
When they could speak at last,
No one wished to hear,
"Don't tell me, it's too awful."
Jew, gentile, all turned away.

No one wanted Lazarus
To rise from the dead.
He was an embarrassment,
Unwelcome reminder
Of things best forgotten.

They learned to be silent,
Buried alive among the corpses
As it had been in the beginning
In the time of the holocaust.

Who Knows Where the Joy Goes

Who knows where the joy goes
Knows we're killing the dolphins
Somewhere far out to sea.

Caught in the tuna nets
The gentle dolphins drown,
They, no man's enemy.
(Go down grace, go down
Freedom.)

Who wakes from a nightmare
Hearing a faint scream
Knows terror at work
Somewhere far away.
(Go down grace, go down
Gentleness.)

Who weeps without reason
In a sudden seizure
Hears a terrible silence
Half the world away.

Is the last dolphin dying?
Is there no friend left?
Are we here alone?

Ut Unium Sint

He climbed the arid steps of power
Simple as any shepherd, whole.
Ignoring pomp, at every hour
Commanded natural being and the soul.
And now together as one family
We mourn a loving father and a son,
And learn the great communion severally,
As witnessed by the shepherd, John.

He shares the heaven of Renoir
On whose last day of pain and fealty
Contorted hands paid homage to a flower,
Painted and blessed the red anemone.
Renoir died praising, John, full of hope,
Through whom love poured with unimpeded force.
Each said, radical painter, radiant pope,
"In the constructive element, immerse!"

An Elegy for Scrabble

Now in the universe
There is a small hole
That Scrabble filled.

I came home with the empty box,
The old speckled cat
"Put to sleep," as they say.

But she was old and ornery,
Often cross, often remote,
I am torn in two. Brutal grief.

At five she woke me
With imperious miaows,
"Where is my breakfast?"

But of all my cats
She of the gold-flecked eyes
Had the most poignant gaze,

A way of looking
That came from deep down
And smote with its sadness.

Goodbye, dear Scrabble,
You took much and gave little,
And perhaps that is why

You were greatly loved.
Black and gold, complaining
Ghost in this house,

Sleep well at last,
And let me also go
From heartbreak to healing.

Cold Spring

The long light on green lawns is given back,
The pattern of the trees set forth on evening air,
But formal through the foam, designed in black.
It is the clarity of spring we see this year.

Would a more clement season perhaps have shown
The way to cleave rock and less cool and strange
Brought up the wild source shouting from the stone?
This held the growing inward and the secret change.

For in this spring you have been that which shone,
Have become simply the pure clarity of light
That shows the trees black on the vivid lawn
And paints the static scene, indelible and bright.

One may behold and yet not suffer change
And the source still be locked from its return:
This love is in the eyes, not yet in the heart's range,
So it is trees and the green lawn that seem to burn.

Intimation

There is nowhere, no corner of a room, no garden,
No time of all times that is isolated, ours.
Between the tension of these actual walls,
We live, and the specific gravity of hours.

But there are instants. Suddenly you are.
I see arrested, sculptured, you set forth
Upon the landscape like a pillar casting
A long shadow to my feet on whirling earth.

Afterwards I remember the sight clearly,
As something unexplained, still strange.
But definite as dream when, upon waking,
The dreamed event becomes incapable of change.

Letters to Myself

1

The terrible fear, the fear of feeling,
Must I hear it defended on every side?
Live like a madman echoing his cell?

The fact is I am whole and very well,
Joyful, centered, not to be turned aside,
Full of healing and of self-healing.

Only the muse does not bid me cease,
Who does not listen and who cannot care,
Has never said "be quiet," uttered harm.

She, the dark angel and the silent charm,
Is all of hope and nothing of despair,
And in her long withholding is my peace.

2

Here joy does live quite close to agony,
But why does everyone see only pain?
Now I am with my deepest self again,
Why are they so afraid, afraid for me?

Who must be changed? Only myself, of course.
But this has always been the work at hand;
I live by its inexorable demand,
And must be changed to reach the deepest source.

Who to be hurt, who to be killed but me?
The phoenix who must burn to die and live.
Who says that through my death I nothing give?
Though I am nothing, the fire is Mystery.

Who cannot see this curious work of grace?
Who tells the poet, "silence, danger here!"
God knows I live each day in greater fear,
And out of agony structure my face

To sustain tension, yet discover poise,
For this Magnificat of severe joys.

The Seed

Once more I lay hurt aside
To go down, down, down
To the deep source,
To the strong seed
Of our passionate love.

The flesh mourns
But it has been sown
With your life,
Your being.
And after two years
Without touch
The seed is still there.
When I see you it stirs—
Seed in an Egyptian tomb
Given sun and water
Crosses two thousand years
And comes alive.

That is the mystery—
The force of what was given,
The fertility in it.

The Consummation

There on your bed lay poetry alive
With all that it can ever hope to give,
And there at last for one transcendent hour
You gave yourself into its gentle power.
Now the long tension slowly falls away
And we may be together in the simple day,
Not lovers, but by loving truly blest,
So take the light, my soul, and let us rest.

There on your bed you held me in your eyes,
Held me alive in your clear quiet gaze,
And even as your voice made strange lament
The light poured out, unfaltering, and sent
Beyond your power to hold it back from me
The shining of your inmost clarity.
Not lovers we, but strangely joined and blest,
So take the soul, my light, and let us rest.

There on your bed lay poetry alone
With all its hungers nourished at the bone,
And all its prayers and its long fierce desire
Held in the cool of your dark, magic fire,
As your cold hand, forgetful as a leaf,
Lay in my hand as if some human grief
Or some long praise could find a home at last,
So take this flesh, my soul, and let us rest.

There on your bed lay poetry beside
Neither a living bridegroom or a bride,
As if we two lay there already dead,
Hands, eyelids, heavier than lead,
And in this consummation, all withheld,
Except the soul upon a shining field,
And all received and given, and all lost—
So take the soul, my flesh, and let us rest.

The Image Is a Garden

My image is this garden in the autumn,
A tangle of late asters, unpruned roses,
Some to be frost-killed, others still to open,
Some failures visible, some wild successes.
The rich disorder sprang from a design
But who can hold full summer to a line?

We have what was planned, and something more,
We have what was planned and something less.
Salvage, invent, re-think and re-explore
The garden-child and the child-wilderness—
Each day I recognize their fealty
To that self whom I slowly learn to free.

This self has lately come to solitude
Who long demanded love as source and prime.
Now the wild garden and the ragged wood,
And the uncharted winter's fallow time
Become the source and the true reservoir:
Look for my love in the autumnal flower.

Index of Titles and First Lines